The Wild World of Animals

Parrots

Colorful Birds

by Fran Howard

Consultant:
Tim Wright
Research Biologist
Smithsonian National Zoo
Washington, D.C.

Bridgestone Books
an imprint of Capstone Press
Mankato, Minnesota

Bridgestone Books are published by Capstone Press
151 Good Counsel Drive, P.O. Box 669, Mankato, Minnesota 56002
www.capstonepress.com

Library of Congress Cataloging-in-Publication Data
Howard, Fran, 1953–
    Parrots: colorful birds / by Fran Howard.
    p. cm.—(The wild world of animals)
    Includes bibliographical references and index.
    Contents: Parrots—Where parrots live—Parrot toes—What parrots eat—Nests—
Chicks—Parrot sounds—Predators—Parrots and people—Hands on: how parrots
crack nuts.
    ISBN-13: 978-0-7368-2615-0 (hardcover)
    ISBN-10: 0-7368-2615-7 (hardcover)
    1. Parrots—Juvenile literature. [1. Parrots.] I. Title. II. Series.
QL696.P7H69 2005
598.7′1—dc22   2003025826

Editorial Credits
Blake A. Hoena, editor; Linda Clavel, designer; Scott Thoms, photo researcher;
    Eric Kudalis, product planning editor

Photo Credits
Corbis/Christophe Loviny, 14; Norbert Schaefer, 20
Derk R. Kuyper, 16
Digital Stock, cover
Minden Pictures/Claus Meyer, 8; Frans Lanting, 10
naturepl.com/Dave Watts, 12; Miles Barton 6
PhotoDisc Inc., 1
Tom Stack & Associates/Dave Watts, 4
Wolfgang Kaehler/www.wkaehlerphoto.com, 18

1 2 3 4 5 6 09 08 07 06 05 04

Table of Contents

wing

bill

tail

green rosella

feet

4

Parrots

Parrots are birds with brightly colored feathers. Many parrots are green, but they can be almost any color. Parrots are between 3.5 and 39 inches (9 and 99 centimeters) tall. About 350 kinds of parrots live in the world.

Parrots' colorful feathers help them blend in with their surroundings. Parrots' feathers look similar to flowers and fruit that grow in rain forests.

rainbow lorikeet

6

Where Parrots Live

Most kinds of parrots live in tropical **rain forests**. Rain forest habitats provide parrots with food and **shelter**. Many parrots live in warm parts of Africa, Asia, Australia, South America, and Central America.

habitat
the place and natural conditions in which an animal lives

red-tailed amazon

8

Parrot Toes

Parrots have two toes on the front and two toes on the back of their feet. Their toes help them hold onto **perches**. Parrots also hold food with their toes. Most other birds do not use their feet to eat.

blue and yellow macaw

What Parrots Eat

Most parrots eat seeds, nuts, and fruit. Parrots use their hook-shaped bills to grab food. Parrots crack open nuts with their bills. Some parrots catch insects to eat.

orange-bellied parrots

Nests

Most parrots make their nests in hollow spaces in trees. Parrots use **natural** holes or holes made by other birds. **Female** parrots lay two to eight eggs in their nests. Adult parrots sit on the eggs to keep them warm.

FUN FACTS

Parrots and other birds have some bones that are hollow. The hollow bones make birds light and allow birds to fly.

14

Chicks

Young parrots are called chicks. Chicks do not have feathers when they **hatch**. Adult parrots feed chicks by chewing up food and then placing it in the chicks' mouths. Young parrots stay in the nest until they grow feathers and can fly.

FUN FACTS

To "parrot" means to copy
what someone else said.

Parrot Sounds

Parrots make many sounds. They squawk, shriek, and hoot. Parrots make sounds to warn each other of danger. They also make sounds to tell other parrots who they are. Pet parrots will copy sounds. They can learn to whistle or say words.

black-capped lory

18

Predators

Adult parrots do not have many natural **predators**. Snakes, wild cats, and monkeys eat parrot chicks. Some people catch wild parrots to sell as pets. In many countries, it is against the law to catch wild parrots. It is illegal to sell wild parrots in the United States.

illegal
against the law

budgerigar

Parrots and People

Many people enjoy parrots. Some people own pet parrots. Pet owners like parrots because they are colorful birds. Some people travel to rain forests to see wild parrots. Many wild parrots are protected in national parks.

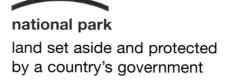

national park
land set aside and protected by a country's government

Hands On: How Parrots Crack Nuts

Parrots have strong bills that can crack open nuts. Try different materials to see how strong parrots' bills are.

What You Need

several hard nuts, such as almonds, still in the shell
2 plastic spoons
2 sticks, about the width of your fingers
metal nut cracker or pliers

What You Do

1. Take one of the nuts and squeeze it between your fingers. Can you crack open its shell?
2. Place a nut between the middle part of the two plastic spoons. Hold the handles of the spoons together with one hand. With the other hand, try to bring the other ends of the spoons together. Does the nut crack?
3. Repeat step 2 using the sticks. Does the nut crack?
4. Now use the metal nut cracker. Can you crack open the nut?

Parrots have hard bills and strong jaw muscles. They can crack open nuts easily with their bills. If a parrot bit a person's finger, the parrot could bite through flesh and bone.

Glossary

female (FEE-male)—an animal of the sex that can give birth to young animals

hatch (HACH)—to break out of an egg; parrots and other birds hatch from eggs.

natural (NACH-ur-uhl)—found in or produced by nature

perch (PURCH)—a bar or branch on which a bird can rest

predator (PRED-uh-tur)—an animal that hunts other animals for food

rain forest (RAYN FOR-ist)—a thick forest where a great deal of rain falls

shelter (SHEL-tur)—a place where animals can stay safe from predators and the weather

Read More

Altman, Linda Jacobs. *Parrots*. Perfect Pets. New York: Benchmark Books/Marshall Cavendish, 2001.

Murray, Julie. *Parrots*. Animal Kingdom. Edina, Minn.: Abdo, 2002.

Rabinowitz, Sima. *Parrots*. Let's Investigate. Mankato, Minn.: Creative Education, 2002.

Internet Sites

FactHound offers a safe, fun way to find Internet sites related to this book. All of the sites on FactHound have been researched by our staff.

Here's how:
1. Visit *www.facthound.com*
2. Type in this special code **0736826157** for age-appropriate sites. Or enter a search word related to this book for a more general search.
3. Click on the **Fetch It** button.

FactHound will fetch the best sites for you!

Index